Information Report on the Assessment of DoD Support to the Iraqi Security Forces Inspectors General (Report No. IE-2008-010) July 31, 2008.

Inspector General

United States
Department *of* Defense

DEPARTMENT OF DEFENSE
OFFICE OF INSPECTOR GENERAL

MISSION STATEMENT

Promote integrity, accountability, and improvement of Department of Defense personnel, programs and operations to support the Department's mission and serve the public interest.

Executive Summary

Inspections & Evaluations

Information Report on the Assessment of DoD Support to the Iraqi Security Forces Inspectors General (Report No. IE-2008-010) July 31, 2008.

What Was Done

This assessment was conducted from March 29, 2007 through August 1, 2007. Assessment activities took place in Washington D.C. and in Iraq from May 8 through June 21, 2007.

The assessment was a self-initiated evaluation of DoD support to assist the Iraqi Ministry of Defence[1] (MoD), the Ministry of Interior (MoI), and Joint Headquarters Inspectors General in establishing a self-sustaining Inspector General (IG) function under Iraqi law. We focused on the operations, plans, and projected needs of these Iraqi Security Forces (ISF) IG organizations within the context of the U.S. Government's transition and capacity-building goals, as well as Iraqi anti-corruption strategies and objectives.

In examining IG capacity-building activities and this assessment report, it is important to keep in mind the distinctions that exist between IG activities at the ministerial or departmental levels, which are generally directed at prevention or detection of fraud, waste, and abuse, and IG activities within military organizations, which generally focus on operational readiness.[2]

This report reflects the state of affairs from March 29, 2007, through August 1, 2007, and does not account for events or developments following those dates. Any material obtained later is identified in explanatory footnotes.

What Was Identified

The DoD-supported program to foster IG development within the ISF was generally well-conceived and delivered in a satisfactory manner.

IG offices have been established at the MoD headquarters and at all appropriate levels in the Iraqi military. IG offices have also been established at the MoI headquarters. An MoI IG provincial presence is evolving and may complement the existing MoI IG structure. Although relatively new in establishment, the Iraqi National Counterterrorism structure also included an IG function.

---

[1] Iraq has adopted the UK-favored spelling for the Ministry as "Defence." Because that spelling appears in the Government of Iraq (GoI)-produced English-language documents regarding the Ministry, we use that spelling throughout this report.

[2] The differences in focus reflect those present in the U.S. systems on which the Iraqi IG systems are modeled.

IG advisory personnel provided by Multi-National Security Transition Command-Iraq (MNSTC-I) were experienced and professional. They were well-received and respected by their Iraqi IG counterparts. Those advisors provided valuable day-to-day mentoring to ISF IG personnel. Advisory personnel had clearly succeeded in conveying the fundamental concepts behind an IG system to their Iraqi counterparts throughout each of the ISF IG offices.

Although the fundamental concepts of economy, efficiency, and integrity, as well as deterring corruption and enhancing organizational performance, were grasped by Iraqi ISF personnel, those concepts were not yet ingrained throughout the ISF. Survival of an ISF IG system requires a sustained multi-year commitment of advisory personnel and training support from DoD.

Considerations for the Future

On the basis of our observations, we identified five considerations which may be of significance for future activities. The considerations are described in detail beginning on page 29 and address the following subjects:

- Support for a centralized Iraqi training academy for the Iraqi national-level anticorruption and oversight organizations.
- Planning for and provision of Iraqi IG support during Iraqi joint police and military operations.
- DoD guidance regarding provision of IG advisory and mentoring activities to host-nation security establishments.
- Continuity of support for IG development within the ISF as it continues to grow and mature.
- Multi-National Forces-Iraq (MNF-I) and MNSTC-I participation in the Embassy Baghdad Anti-Corruption Working Group and their assistance in developing a comprehensive coalition anti-corruption strategy.

MEMORANDUM FOR COMMANDER, U.S. CENTRAL COMMAND
COMMANDER, MULTI-NATIONAL FORCE – IRAQ
COMMANDER, MULTI-NATIONAL SECURITY TRANSITION
 COMMAND – IRAQ
COMMANDER, MULTI-NATIONAL CORPS – IRAQ

July 31, 2008

SUBJECT: Information Report on Assessment of DoD Support to Iraqi Security Forces Inspectors General (Report No. IE-2008-010)

We are providing this assessment report for your information and use. We assessed DoD support being provided to development of Iraqi Security Forces Inspectors General. This assessment was made in order that appropriate action could be taken and to provide a baseline assessment to inform future examination of the subject, if appropriate. The assessment team included personnel experienced in the development of inspector general systems.

We discussed the results of this project assessment with representatives of Multi-National Forces-Iraq, Multi-National Corps-Iraq, and Multi-National Security Transition Command-Iraq. This report includes no recommendations that require management comments; therefore, we are publishing this report in final form.

We acknowledge that many changes, such as a revamp of the Multi-National Security Transition Command-Iraq Iraqi Security Force Inspector General advisory structure, movement of the Iraqi Ministry of Defense Inspector General Human Rights Directorate to the Ministry of Defense General Counsel Office, and the addition of significant numbers of personnel to all Iraqi Security Force Inspectors General offices have taken place since the closing date of this report. The effect of those and other changes on the subject matter of this assessment is left to such subsequent assessments as may be undertaken.

We appreciate courtesies extended to our staff. This letter does not require a formal response. If you have questions, please contact Mr. John G. Townsend at (703) 604-8956 or Mr. Deane Williams at (703) 604-9152. See Appendix F for the report distribution.

Thomas F. Gimble
Principal Deputy

GENERAL INFORMATION

Forward questions or comments concerning the Information Report on Assessment of Department of Defense Support to the Iraqi Security Forces Inspectors General and other activities conducted by the Inspections & Evaluations Directorate to:

Inspections & Evaluations Directorate
Office of the Deputy IG for Policy & Oversight
Office of IG of the Department of Defense
400 Army Navy Drive
Arlington, Virginia 22202-4704
crystalfocus@dodig.mil

An overview of the IG of the Department of Defense mission and organizational structure is available at http://www.dodig.mil.

TO REPORT FRAUD, WASTE, AND ABUSE, OR MISMANAGEMENT

Contact the DoD OIG Hotline by telephone at (800) 424-9098, by e-mail at hotline@dodig.mil or in writing:

Defense Hotline
The Pentagon
Washington, D.C.
20301-1900

TABLE OF CONTENTS

List of Appendixes

Introduction

The assessment was conducted from March 29, 2007, through August 1, 2007. Assessment activities took place in Iraq from May 8 through June 21, 2007. The Assessment team visited the following Baghdad vicinity locations: Camp Victory; the International Zone, including the Iraqi Ministry of Defence[1] (MoD) Headquarters Building; Forward Operating Base (FOB) Honor; Old Muthana Air Base; FOB Shield; Baghdad Police College; and the Ministry of Interior (MoI) Headquarters building in the Rusafa district. Other Iraq locations visited were the 10th Iraqi Army Division Headquarters at Basra, Taji Air Base/National Depot, and the Iraqi Naval Base at Umm Qsar. The team conducted research, analyses, and follow-up activities in Washington D.C. prior to and after the field work.

DoD Office of the Inspector General (IG) personnel who contributed to this assessment were:

> Mr. Deane Williams
>
> Mr. John G. Townsend
>
> COL (P) Nickolas P. Tooliatos, USAR

Mr. Townsend and COL (P) Tooliatos conducted the field work in Iraq.

This report reflects the state of affairs during the period of March 29 through August 1, 2007, and does not account for events or developments following the concluding date. Any material we later obtained is identified in explanatory footnotes.

Since then, the team monitored the DoD-supported program designed to assist the growth of IG offices at the MoD headquarters and at all appropriate levels in the Iraqi military[2], as well as the IG offices at the MoI headquarters and in the Iraqi National Counter-terrorism (CT) Task Force. A MoI IG provincial presence and structure, while under consideration by the MoI IG, is unsettled and not likely to be clarified until a provincial powers law is enacted. Although newly established, the CT structure also included an IG function.

Effective linkages between the developed ministerial or national IG entities and the developing subordinate or provincial entities were not yet mature in either the ISF IG systems or in the coalition IG advisory organizations. Planned transition of MNSTC-I to an Office of Security Cooperation and transitions of authority to succeeding U.S. corps headquarters to perform the MNC-I mission will require vigilance from all concerned to ensure that momentum in the development of the ISF IG systems is maintained.

---

[1] Iraq has adopted the UK-favored spelling for the Ministry as "Defence." Because that spelling appears in the Government of Iraq (GoI)-produced English-language documents regarding the Ministry, we use that spelling throughout this report.

[2] The differences in focus reflect those present in the U.S. systems on which the Iraqi IG systems are modeled.

At the time of this assessment, the MNSTC-I organization did not have an IG position.[3] During field work, we identified the need to formally create an IG position at the MNSTC-I staff level in order to coordinate IG advisory and training issues, both inside and outside the command. The Commander, MNSTC-I acted immediately upon the suggestion. The position was created and filled by a United States Marine Corps IG-qualified colonel who proved to be value-added in building capacity for the IG offices within the Iraqi security ministries and in supporting the overall anti-corruption efforts.

It is noteworthy that every Iraqi security ministry and military IG or IG office employee we talked to described the IG function as being the eyes, ears, and conscience of its minister (or commander). Although the building blocks of an effective system were in place, the concepts of an IG system are so radically different from the experiences of most ISF personnel that it will require years of sustained attention to effectively inculcate IG values and to build effective IG systems.

Resourcing was a serious issue in both the Iraqi MoI and MoD IG offices. Lack of access to transportation, office space, and technology hindered operations in all offices. Training and security impediments were also major concerns. MoI IG had fewer than 20 percent of authorized personnel and no realistic plan to correct the shortfall.

In Iraq, the Embassy's interagency working groups served to integrate the anti-corruption plans and IG advisory activities of Multi-National Forces-Iraq (MNF-I) with those of U.S. Mission-Iraq (USM-I). MNF-I and its subordinate elements must do more than observe if the work of those groups is to be effective. Given the experience and resources DoD can provide, MNF-I should seek to have a prominent role in the Anti-Corruption Working Group and any like entities. According to a Special IG for Iraq Reconstruction (SIGIR), MNF-I senior officers should be involved with the Anti-Corruption Working Group. We concur with this recommendation.

MNSTC-I advisors instructed or facilitated many outstanding one-of-a-kind ISF IG training events. These training events were ad hoc and not institutionalized. A number of "stove-piped" training courses to teach IG-type skills were being created, some in or for the ISF. The most effective and economical approach to inculcating IG values and to sustain, professionalize, and coordinate Iraqi IG/anti-corruption/good governance systems in Iraq is to establish an Iraqi national training entity. Such an initiative has been endorsed repeatedly by the Iraqi leadership.

While DoD may not have the U.S. lead for this initiative, DoD activities and resources should be directed toward supporting the Iraqi Association of Inspectors' General "Academy of Principled Governance" or a similar multi-ministry Iraqi national training entity. MNSTC-I should seek to integrate standardized training programs into a national-level, multi-ministry IG and Anti-Corruption Academy program to assist in building an enduring Iraqi anti-corruption system.

---

[3] Shortly after the completion of this assessment, MNSTC-I established an IG position.

Iraqi Objectives for Iraqi IG Systems

Iraq Federal IG System:[4]

- "Stable IG system that complements the CPI[5] and BSA.[6]

- Sustainable IG system supported by permanent training mechanism for ethics, leadership, advanced auditing, inspections, and investigations.

- Professional IG system with highly trained staffs, operating under SOPs for day-to-day operations, with published government and ministry standards to reference their operations."

Iraqi Security Forces IG Systems[7]

MoD IG: "Monitor MoD levels of performance according to standards for the purposes of development, fighting administrative and financial corruption, and preventing violations of human rights according to international standards."[8]

MoI IG: "The IG acts as an independent and objective monitoring office in the MoI, and conducts, supervises, monitors, and initiates audits, inspections, and investigations related to programs and operations of the MoI. The primary focus of the IG is to provide accountability, integrity, and performance review in order to prevent, deter, and identify fraud, waste, abuse, corruption, illegal activity, and human rights violations."[9]

JHQ/Military IGs: "[To] achieve operational readiness and improve the economy and compliance with Human Rights Conventions and fighting corruption and restoring the trust and confidence of the people in the military establishment of the Joint Forces."[10]

Iraqi National Counter-terrorism Task Force IG. At the time of our visit, this IG was newly established--its mission had not yet been developed.

---

[4] From briefing by Dr. Ali Alq, Secretary of the Iraqi Council of Ministers, March 2007.
[5] Commission on Public Integrity was created by CPA Order 55. See Appendix B.
[6] Board of Supreme Audit was created by CPA Order 77. See Appendix B.
[7] From Iraqi Mission Statements.
[8] Briefing by the MoD IG, June 2007.
[9] MoI Strategic Directive 07, p. 2-3-5.
[10] Minister of Defence Directive, 8/19/2006.

Support to Iraqi Security Forces Inspectors General

> "Iraqi IGs are like a ship in a stormy sea…we need all the help we can get."
>
> Senior ISF IG official, Baghdad, June 2007

Recognizing the importance of the role of IGs to the overall anti-corruption, good governance, and rule of law efforts in Iraq, the U.S. Government and its coalition partners have assisted the Government of Iraq (GoI) establish a national IG system. See Appendix B for a brief description of the GoI. DoD provides support to the IGs of the Iraqi Ministry of Defence (MoD), Ministry of Interior (MoI), Joint Headquarters (JHQ)/Military, and the Iraqi National Counter-terrorism Task Force (CT).

Direct Support

The Department of Defense provided personnel to advise and mentor the ISF IG effort. Initially, one DoD civilian was detailed to the Coalition Provisional Authority (CPA) to develop the Iraqi IG system. Since then, three DoD IG civilians have provided advisory or instructional assistance in Baghdad.

Advisory support for ISF IG development efforts flowed first through the CPA, and then through the Embassy's Iraq Reconstruction Management Office. Since late 2005, the ISF advisory mission was conducted primarily through the Multi-National Security and Transition Command-Iraq (MNSTC-I). See Appendix C for a brief description of MNSTC-I. Beginning in 2006, assignment or attachment of military personnel and placement of contractor personnel[11] to the MNSTC-I Transition Teams has provided additional advisory manpower for this mission.

During our assessment, one military officer position was added to the Multi-National Corps-Iraq (MNC-I) IG Joint Manning Document—an advisors position dedicated to the nascent military IG system in the Iraqi Ground Forces Command and its divisions. See Appendix D for a brief description of MNC-I.

At the end of our Iraq field work, there were 13 personnel assigned to IG advisory duties in MNSTC-I. Figure 1 shows the MNSTC-I advisory structure for ISF IGs.

---

[11] MPRI has been the primary source for contractors serving as advisors to ISF IGs.

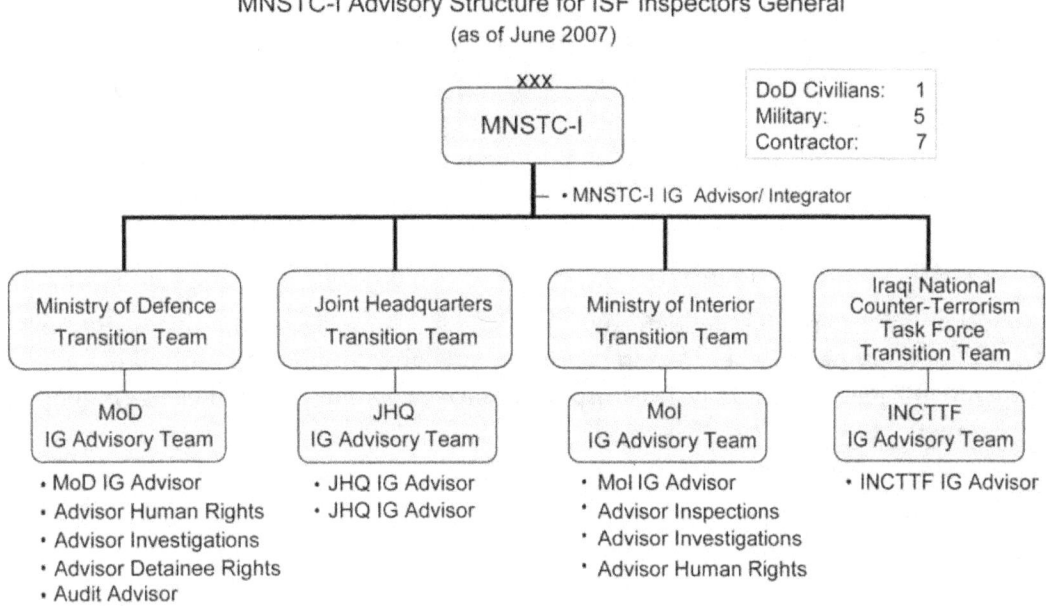

Figure 1: MNSTC-I Advisory Structure for ISF IGs.

Indirect Support

DoD provided indirect support to the ISF IG system. For example, in 2005, the DoD IG planned and facilitated a MoD IG visit to the United States. The Iraqi MoD IG spoke to the President's Council on Integrity and Efficiency, seeking support for the Iraqi IG system.

Additionally, on at least three occasions, the DoD IG or Acting IG met with the full body of 31 Iraqi IGs in Baghdad to discuss topics of common concern and to express his support for the Iraqi IGs.

The DoD has also supported the ISF IG training opportunities at the U.S. Army IG School and facilitated the translation of instructional materials.

Moreover, the DoD extended the Iraq tour of a DoD IG civilian to help coordinate the transition of an incoming Department of State employee who was assigned to advise and mentor the non-security ministry IGs.

To maximize the effectiveness of advice to the ISF IGs, in 2004 the DoD IG established a "Reachback Cell" in Washington D.C. to support deployed personnel serving as advisors. The cell provided doctrinal support and assistance and conducted research to assist the IG advisors in-theater.

Ministry of Defence Inspector General

Mission: "Monitoring MoD levels of performance according to standards for the purposes of development, fighting administrative and financial corruption, and preventing violations of human rights according to international standards."[1]

Structure

At the time of our visit, the federal-level MoD IG mission was accomplished through an IG office with four operational directorates: Human Rights, Investigations, Audit, and Inspections[2]. The Human Rights Directorate was responsible for oversight of detainee operations and issues for the ministry.

The MoD IG was an officer in the Iraqi Army. The Deputy IG and subordinate Directors were either brigadier generals or civilian equivalents. The IG reported that his office had a mix of 70 civilian and military personnel.

MoD IG Organizational Chart

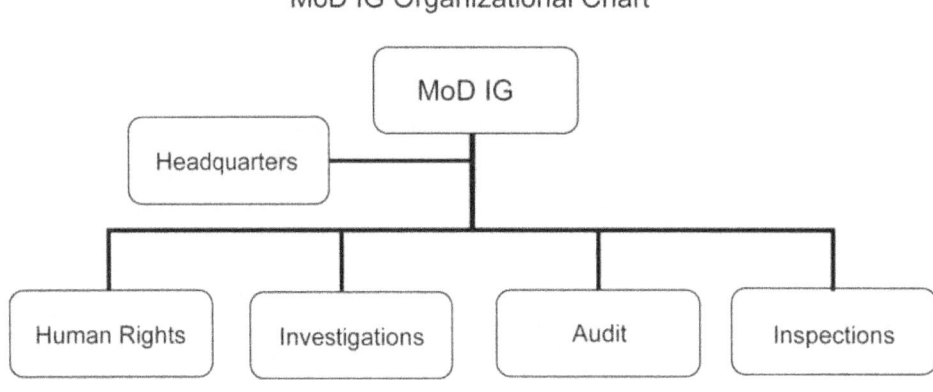

Figure 2. MoD IG Organizational Chart. (Source: Iraqi MoD IG.)

Background of MoD OIG

The following factors are significant to understand the operating environment of the MoD IG.

The first MoD IG was appointed in June 2004, just before the dissolution of the Coalition Provisional Authority and transfer of authority to Iraq. She died of gunshot wounds in October 2005. Soon after her death, the Minister of Defence dismissed the civilian deputy who was acting as IG and ordered the IG office to cease operations. The minister stopped all audits and investigations and denied IG personnel access to any MoD documents. The minister ultimately

---

[1] Briefing by the MoD IG, June 2007
[2] The Human Rights Directorate was added in February 2006 and has since been moved to the MoD Office of General Counsel.

reconsidered his decision and re-instated IG office. Advisory personnel, coalition leaders, and some Iraqis serving in the MoD convinced the Minister of Defence that Iraqi law mandated the function.

This episode illustrates the type of turmoil associated with the fledgling ISF IGs—turmoil that was also common among the non-security IG organizations.

After those events, a serving military officer was appointed as Acting MoD IG and he presided over a period during which time the primary activity was directed at survival of the MoD IG office, rather than pursuing inspections, investigations, and audits.

The next MoD IG was a serving military officer who was the chief of staff for the Chief of the Joint Staff and was generally regarded as a capable IG. He was dismissed by the Minister in May 2007. That dismissal precipitated controversy over whether the removal process followed the law, which requires the existence of cause for dismissing IGs.

The third permanent IG was also a serving Iraqi Army officer and he assumed the position while our team was in Iraq. We noted that he had not met the MNF-I Joint Area Support Group vetting criteria for security badging and, therefore, he required escorted access within the International Zone in Baghdad.

In summary, the two civilians appointed as the MoD IG, one died in 2005, and her acting successor was relieved of duties and replaced. Each of the subsequent acting or permanent MoD IGs were serving military officers.

Advisory Structure

The MoD advisory team was led by a DoD civilian hired specifically to perform the mission. He was a retired military officer with experience working on Provincial Reconstruction Teams in Iraq. He was aided by three experienced team members. Two of these team members were contractors—one was a military reserve officer with a PhD, and the other was a retired U.S. Secret Service agent with IG experience. A U.S. Air Force officer was the third member. The advisory team was very well-regarded by their Iraqi counterparts. One advisor worked primarily with the IG, another worked primarily with Investigations, and two advisors were assigned to advise the Human Rights Directorate. A military officer to advise the Audit Directorate was also slated to begin duties.

Observations

DoD has supported the evolution of the MoD IG capacity building process and has provided experienced and highly qualified advisors. Given the history of an active IG system in the DoD and all branches of the military services, advisors and mentors who have U.S. military backgrounds are generally familiar with the IG system and are able to appreciate the desired end state. Advisors and mentors from other coalition countries or those with non-military backgrounds often are not familiar with concepts fundamental to IG systems.

Given the comparatively small size of the MoD IG office, the advisory process has yielded a relatively mature office with considerable potential. The size of the IG staff has fluctuated around 50 to 70 people throughout its existence. However, the IG organization has benefited from the relative stability of the four senior managers of the directorates—all of whom have been with MoD IG since 2004 and three of whom have been in the same positions. Personnel changes at the Ministry and IG level, coupled with the risky security environment, have constrained the capacity building progress of the MoD IG.

A detailed examination of the actual work in MoD IG showed that a significant proportion of activity was related to contracts—mostly pre-contract reviews, rather than post-contract execution. A proposal to create a single office to deconflict and synchronize the efforts of Audit and Investigations, focusing on integrity within the contracting process, was mentioned in conversation with Iraqi staff members.

The MoD is located in the International Zone adjacent to MNSTC-I Headquarters. Pedestrian travel between MNSTC-I and the MoD is the norm. The short distance makes it easy for the advisors to work with the MoD IG staff. The Iraqi military provides security for the MoD compound and the headquarters building. The MoD IG offices were equipped with computers and office furniture adequate for the complement of MoD IG personnel. However, the IG space was not adequate to accommodate the authorized number of personnel, and there were no plans to disperse MoD IG personnel to additional locations.

Removal of Former IG. During this assessment, the Iraqi Minister of Defence removed his MoD IG. The IG, with support from the Association of Iraqi IGs and some members of the Council of Representatives, resisted the removal. Before the dispute was resolved, the Minister selected a replacement IG who moved into the IG's office and assumed his duties.

In deference to sensitivities of the situation, our assessment team did not get involved in the dispute. When the situation was clarified, the MNSTC-I advisors arranged an appointment with the newly installed IG. We were advised that, unlike the dismissed IG, the new IG met frequently with the Minister. We also learned that the Minister and his designee served together in the old Iraqi Army.

According to the CPA Order 57, "an inspector may be removed by the relevant Minister only for cause. . .and the grounds for removal must be reported to the [Iraqi] Administrator. . . ." Indications suggest that the Minister did not comply with this law. It appears the Minister and the new IG had a good relationship, one founded on a relationship of personal trust. Culturally, trust is an important attribute. The new IG planned to go forward with IG operations appropriate to the level of resources available and appeared to have the Minister's confidence.

New IG Comments. The new IG spoke with our team and expressed gratitude and appreciation for the advisory effort. He articulated his plan to work with MoD employees to teach them to respect the rule of law. He stated that his vision was to educate MoD employees to inculcate appropriate values. He believed his leaders should set the example for others to follow. He acknowledged that he had about 70 employees—about half of his authorization—and that he needed trained, experienced, and professional auditors, investigators, and inspectors.

The IG acknowledged that intimidation affected his staff. He estimated that his employees were only functioning at about 50 percent of their capacity. Although that stymied progress, he assessed that his people were achieving small victories every day.

Audit. MoD IG Audit leadership pointed out with pride that a database had been established and procedures had been implemented to track salaries within MoD. There were scheduled audits of the military salary system, units and bases, and the MoD headquarters administrative functions.

The Audit Directorate did not engage in the same range of audit activities usually encountered in a U.S government department or agency. Instead, the MoD IG audit personnel examined 800 - 1000 contract transactions per month. These examinations primarily centered on reviews of contract documents to confirm that basic contractual provisions were present and to screen for obvious flaws, such as the omission of contract specifications for the delivery of goods or services.

Investigations. Activities of the Investigations Directorate largely related to legal review of MoD contracts. There was an administrative section that pre-screened potential investigations and an investigations section that focused on bribes, nepotism,[3] and theft of public funds.

Among the senior members of the Investigations Directorate there were half dozen lawyers. We noted that the IG Investigations office concentrated on contract-related activity. Although the MNSTC-I advisor had conducted investigative training, the office limited their work to possible criminal wrongdoing involving contractual matters. As illustrated later, the uniformed military IG system was not structured to perform investigations into allegations of criminal conduct and the guidance regarding the responsibilities of the uniformed IGs did not include the criminal investigatory function. Consequently, the Investigations Directorate's narrow focus may be creating a gap in capabilities of the MoD IG.

Inspections. The Inspections Directorate leaders regarded inspections as the "face" of the IG because the inspectors went to military units and bases and inspected other MoD elements. The organization had a 5-year plan with clearly drafted goals and objectives. The focus of the plan was to train the staff and develop their skills. Directorate leaders explained that the staff conducted follow-ups on every inspection and recommended remedies to promote compliance. We observed that there was an active internal and external training program.

Historically, it is interesting to note that there was a very active military inspections program in the former military. And a number of military officers made the point that in the former army, the ranking inspector was a very powerful figure. Apparently, under the old military inspections program, the audit and investigations functions were either subsumed within inspections or were not conducted within the former military structure.

The "default setting" for all of the military officers in any part of the ISF IG systems, and especially in the MoD and the Iraqi military, was a compliance inspection regime, whatever the label given to the event at hand or the assigned responsibilities of the officer. Conversations with many of the military personnel assigned to MoD IG revealed substantial experience as inspectors in the former military. The Director of Inspections in the MoD IG office was a serving Iraqi Army brigadier general.

---

[3] In this context, the assessment team understood the meaning of "nepotism" to be awarding contract based on relationship rather than fair competition.

Human Rights. Two advisors were assigned to the Human Rights Directorate. Both were very capable and passionate about their work with their Iraqi counterparts. The Iraqi director and her staff were quite active in examining MoD-operated detention facilities. It was clear that they took their jobs very seriously.

During our assessment, operations in support of the Baghdad security plan[4] resulted in a large number of prisoners that were apprehended and detained. The accomplishments of the MoD IG Human Rights Director and her advisors were noteworthy in coordinating and collaborating detainee activities among Coalition Task Force 134, MoI and MoD organizations, the Iraqi judiciary, and other GoI entities. The Human Rights staff was out front and conducted oversight visits to check compliance with detainee policies. The MoD Human Rights Directorate was the most active of the ISF IG directorates we observed.

Summary

The MoD IG was the most developed among the ISF IG offices. The Inspections and Human Rights directorates were more active than Investigations and Audit. Given the modest number of authorized personnel and the experience and stability of the directorate's leadership, the MoD IG was more capable of independent operations than other ISF IG offices.

> "We often forget or underestimate the courage and dedication of so many Iraqis... everyday. They and their families risked their lives simply to come to work."
>
> COL Richard Hatch, former MNSTC-JAG,
> (Interview, Contemporary Operations Study Team,
> Combat Studies Institute,
> Fort Leavenworth, KS,
> February 14, 2006.)

---

[4] Operation Fardh al-Qanoon (FAQ).

Joint Headquarters/Military Inspectors General

Mission. "[To] achieve operational readiness and improve the economy and compliance with Human Rights Conventions and fighting corruption and restoring the trust and confidence of the people in the military establishment of the Joint Forces."[5]

Structure

Although Coalition Provisional Authority Order 57 established federal IGs within ministries, it did not address a military IG system or any system for inspections and/or assistance within the military.

In August 2006, the MoD IG and the Director of the Iraqi Joint Staff, together with their advisors, published the MoD Directive to create the military IG system. The directive established a decentralized IG system with IGs at the Joint Headquarters, the services and major commands, and at the Iraqi Army divisions. Regardless of the organizational level, the directive specified that the IGs work for their commanders. However, to facilitate communications among IGs, the directive included provisions for an IG technical (communications) channel to connect the system from the MoD and Joint Forces IGs to the IGs at subordinate levels.

Organizationally, military inspectors[6] focused on combat readiness; whereas the MoD IG generally focused on anti-corruption, human rights, investigations, and audits.

The MoD Directive authorized military IGs for the Joint Headquarters and each of the services' headquarters--Air Force, Navy, Iraqi Ground Forces Command, and the Iraqi Special Operations Forces. In addition, military IGs were allocated to the Assistant Chief of Staff (ACOS) for Support, the ACOS for Training and Doctrine, and to each of the Army Divisions. At the time of our field work, the Tables of Organization and Equipment were pending approval. The proposed personnel allocations in the military IG system range from 26 in the JHQ to 5 in the Iraqi Ground Forces Command and 3 for each Army division, and 3 each for the Iraqi Special Operations Forces, the Air Force, and the Navy. See Table 1.

---

[5] Minister of Defence Directive, 8/19/2006.

[6] The Iraqis use the term "military inspector" to refer to the staff of the military IGs.

Trained Military Inspectors by Service/Command		
Organization/Unit	Recommended Authorized	Trained
Joint Headquarters	26	10
Iraqi Air Force	3	7
Iraqi Navy	3	2
Iraq Special Ops Forces	3	2
ACOS SUPPORT	4	5
ACOS Training & Doctrine	3	1
Iraqi Security Forces Cmd	5	8
1 Iraqi Army Division (IAD)	3	1
2 IAD	3	2
3 IAD	3	4
4 IAD	3	3
5 IAD	3	3
6 IAD	3	6
7 IAD	3	4
8 IAD	3	6
9 IAD	3	6
10 IAD	3	6

Table 1. Trained Military Inspectors by Organization/Unit.
(Source: MNSTC-I JHQ-TT OIG Advisors, 2007.)

Background of JHQ OIG

As described above, the MoD Directive established the military IG system to include the Joint Headquarters Office of the Inspector General. Several factors should be considered to understand the creation of the JHQ OIG.

First, according to Iraqi officials, one of the MoD objectives was to achieve an approximate 80 percent civilian and 20 percent military mix of personnel in the "civilian" organization and embed some Iraqi civilian officials in the Joint Headquarters "military" staff. This "mix" was to apply to the MoD IG, as well as other MoD components. The thought was to foster civil-military relations and transparency as this new Iraqi institution evolved.

Second, even though a formal plan was not written, the vision of the first MoD IG was to initially achieve a functional ministry-level IG operation. While doing so, her plan was to observe the qualities of military officers—colonels and brigadier generals—assigned to the MoD IG and select those who understood and embraced the principles of the IG system as the leaders for the military IG system.

Thirdly, a number of events—the untimely death of the first IG in 2005, the subsequent break in rapport with the former Minister, and turnover in ministers with subsequent changes in the government—impacted original vision of how a military IG system for the JHQ, the services, and subordinate organizations would be developed.

Finally, in late summer of 2006, the Minister of Defence exercised his authority and directed the creation of a Military IG system. In July 2006, the Chief of Staff, Joint Forces selected the Commander of the 1st Iraqi Army Division to become the first IG of the Joint Headquarters. The Minister of Defence and Prime Minister approved the nomination.

A series of military IG qualification courses played a significant role in the selection and training of personnel for this system.

First Qualification Course—November 12-28, 2006. The concept for the first qualification course was approved by the MoD IG and Chief of Staff, Joint Forces, prior to the appointment of the JHQ IG. The course served several purposes. Primarily, it established an incentive to press for an appointment of a military IG and the selection of officers to attend training and fill positions within the military inspector general system. Advisors prepared each block of instruction based on U.S. Army IG University course materials, modified the materials to meet the needs of the Iraqi system, facilitated the translation process, and pre-briefed the JHQ IG-designee. The designee played a key role in organizing the course and coordinating the content of the materials. Sixty students started the course--52 graduated. MNSTC-I advisors conducted most of the instruction. The Iraqi military provided logistical support. The course was considered highly successful.

Second Qualification Course—March 11-29, 2007. The second qualification course was modeled on the first, except that it was entirely planned, taught, and supported by the Iraqis. The JHQ IG and his deputy were very much involved in coordinating the course details. Selected graduates from the first course served as the principal instructors. Forty-two officers, primarily from Army divisions, graduated. According to the advisors, the course was more successful than the first and the presentations and content were excellent.

Advisory Structure

The senior advisor to the JHQ IG was a newly arrived Navy captain. The second member of the JHQ/Military advisory team was a contractor who was a retired military officer with previous IG assignments and experience. Both appeared capable and experienced. They were challenged to provide advice to the JHQ IG, as well as the Navy and Air Force IGs.

The advisors operated primarily at the MoD Headquarters building, since the JHQ and Air Force IGs were collocated in the same facility. The IGs had very crowded, shared office space in the main MoD building with very spartan overflow space in temporary structures in the rear courtyard of the MoD HQ.

Observations

Although the aggressive training program for military IGs has provided qualified IG personnel, approval of staffing and equipment authorization documents have lagged. Military Inspectors work for their commanders, but use an IG technical channel for communications between MoD IG and division inspectors.

The Iraqi Armed Forces had a long tradition of inspections, but the former military IG system was centralized at the headquarters and the inspectors were empowered to reward and punish.

The new system of decentralized inspectors gives lower commanders a powerful tool--but the problem is that commanders do not yet understand how to use the tool effectively. To help remedy this problem, the JHQ IG visited many of the units and their newly trained military inspectors and informed commanders on how to use his IG.

Iraqi senior military leaders claimed the decentralized military inspector system would take about two years from inception to prove valuable; otherwise it might revert to a centralized model. To sustain the decentralized system, commander and senior staff education is essential.

Developing the capacity to staff detailed plans has been challenging for an Iraqi military establishment accustomed to following direct orders from above. To help overcome this challenge, MNSTC-I advisors provided draft operational directives and policies which were patterned on U.S. Army Regulation 20-1, "Inspector General Activities and Procedures." The JHQ IG's office used the drafts for reference to develop its own Standard Operating Procedures (SOPs) and policies. The JHQ IG office was distributing those SOPs and policies to the services, major commands, and division inspectors.

Activity

The JHQ IG visited subordinate echelons to ensure inspectors were properly positioned and equipped, and were conducting inspections. The IG had visited Air Force, Iraqi Special Operations Forces, IGFC, ACOS Support, ACOS Training & Doctrine, and four divisions. At the time of our field work, the IG was planning to visit the remaining divisions and the Navy. He used the visits to discuss with commanders the role of the military inspectors and to identify future training and inspection needs and policy or structure changes.

Our team accompanied the JHQ IG on visits to Iraqi military units, which were largely familiarization and orientation visits. Similarly, we accompanied the Air Force IG on a unit visit.

Summary

The JHQ and military IG system at all levels is evolving. Qualified advisors are needed to help the Iraqis build a sustainable IG institution. The development of advisory linkages between MNSTC-I and MNC-I will further assist the Iraqi military in integrating IG efforts in their MoD and military systems.

> "...the former regime fostered inefficiency and corruption in Iraqi governmental institutions...a concerted effort is needed to restore public trust and confidence in these institutions."
>
> From the preamble to CPA Order 57, which created the Federal Iraqi IG system

Ministry of the Interior Inspector General

Mission: "The IG acts as an independent and objective monitoring office in the MoI that conducts, supervises, monitors, and initiates audits, inspections and investigations related to programs and operations of the MOI. The primary focus of the IG is to provide accountability, integrity, and performance review in order to prevent, deter, and identify fraud, waste, abuse, corruption, illegal activity and human rights violations."[7]

Structure

As depicted in Figure 3, the MoI IG office was organized with administrative support functions and three Director Generals--Administration and Finance, Audits, and Investigations and Human Rights. Also, the chart shows that 15 Provincial IG Offices report to MoI IG. At the time of our visit, the management personnel had been designated and were in place, but the final MOI IG staff structure was not yet "approved," although it had been sent to the minister for approval.

Given the wide range of activities and responsibilities under the MOI, the IG Directorate was a large organization dealing with complex issues. The IG advised us that he was authorized 5,000 employees.

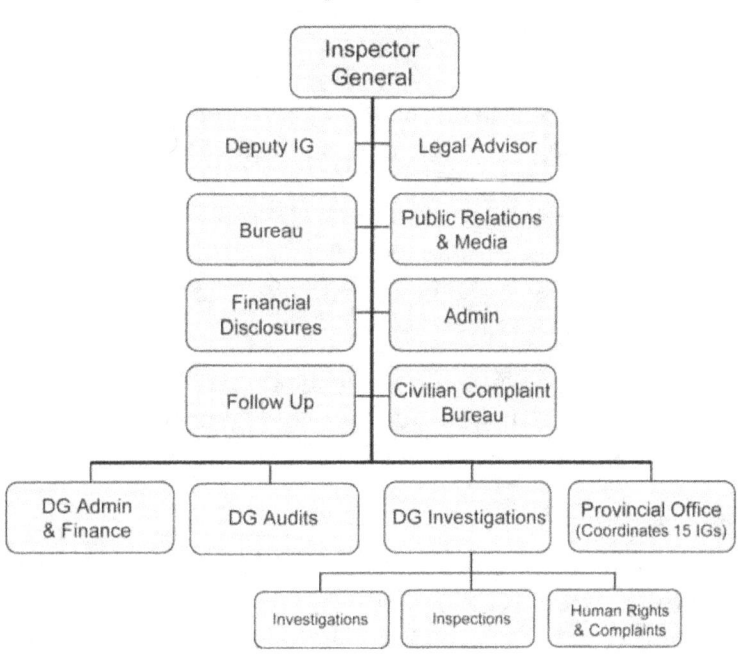

Figure 3: MoI OIG Organizational Chart. (Source: MNSTCI-I MOI-TT Advisors)

---

[7] MoI Strategic Directive 07, p 2-3-5.

Background of the Ministry of Interior Inspector General office

Prior to the dissolution of CPA, the then-serving Minister of the Interior dismissed the CPA-selected IG for his ministry. The CPA Administrator ordered the dismissal reversed but the Minister did not comply by the time CPA transferred authority to the Iraqi government. The controversy continued into 2005 and eventually resulted in a court order restoring the dismissed IG to his position. The order was not enforced and ultimately the dismissed IG abandoned efforts to return to the position.

On December 25, 2005, the Minister re-established the MoI Internal Affairs Directorate (IA) and transferred a large part of investigative capacity out of the MoI IG to IA. Consequently, this realignment severely reduced the capacity for the MoI IG to conduct investigative operations.

At the time of our visit, the incumbent IG had been serving since his appointment in January 2006. He took an active role in the organization and he developed the IG's mission statement and defined the functions for the IG office.

The incumbent Minister's focus was to improve attention to human rights. The MoI IG's Human Rights directorate appeared to be among the most active element, pursuing an ongoing program to observe and report on MoI detainee operations.

On March 16, 2007, the Minister suspended all operations of the MoI IG office—which was done when the IG was out of country visiting his family. We were told that the Minister perceived the tone of a letter from the Acting IG to be disrespectful.

In April 2007, the Minister's suspension of IG operations was rescinded. However, the IG was required to return MOI employees who were on temporary OIG assignments back to their parent offices. He was also directed to consolidate his inspectors with those working in 22 other MoI offices. It was reported that the IG returned over 500 employees (40% of his workforce). At the time of our field work, approximately 850 employees, from a total authorization of 5,000, provided oversight, inspections, and investigations to the Iraq-wide MoI organization of over 300,000 personnel.

The MoI IG was developing a hiring/training/equipping plan which he said would significantly grow his organization. In April 2007, the MoI OIG began receiving its first independent budget funds directly from the Ministry of Finance.[8]

Advisory Structure

During our visit, a contractor led the four-person MoI IG advisory team. He was a retired military officer with previous IG experience, both as a military officer and as a DoD civilian. As a contractor, he had recently advised foreign military IGs elsewhere in the Middle East. From all observations and accounts, he was a very capable and experienced advisor. We noted that he had a very professional and respectful working relationship with the IG and his staff.

---

[8] Receipt of funds by all ministerial IGs directly from the Ministry of Finance, rather than through the Ministerial budget allocation, is intended to afford IGs a degree of independence from the ministries for which they have oversight responsibility.

Also assigned to MoI IG advisory team was one military officer and two other contractors. All three had credible experience and qualifications. In addition to compliments on their work voiced by Iraqi personnel, we observed all advisors had a satisfactory working relationship with their Iraqi counterparts.

Observations

Location. The MOI advisors worked in the 10-story MoI headquarters building, which is adjacent to the Forward Operating Base Shields in the Rusafa district of Baghdad.[9] The headquarters compound included detention facilities for more than 5,000 Iraqi prisoners, Iraqi court facilities, and ancillary functions of the courts. Hence, the MoI compound was considered the "Rule of Law Green Zone." Baghdad Police College was nearby and contiguous to FOB Shield. The MoI IG advisors lived on the coalition-controlled FOB and had limited office space on the FOB compound.

During our visit, most interviews with MoI IG personnel and advisors, as well as observation of direct advisory activity, took place at the MoI HQ building.

MoI Provincial Presence. During discussions with directorate-level Iraqi officials, we learned that visits to provincial MoI offices were being planned and scheduled, so that recommendations for structure and manning levels could be formulated. We were told that this was to be the first effort to coordinate and communicate with MoI IG offices in the provinces.

Given the MoI's responsibilities, execution at the provincial level is integral to the Ministry's mission. We determined that the success of the effort at the local level will largely depend on the participation of advisors and mentors at the provincial office locations—and to what extent this support can be provided by the coalition military or provincial reconstruction teams. We contend that there is a definite role for advisors and mentors.

Also, we were told that provincial IG officials and judges are intimated because of their role in exposing and prosecuting fraud, waste, and abuse. Their personal safety and the safety of their families are at risk. Strategies to mitigate these risks are important if there is to be any positive impact from provincial MoI IG representatives as they work to combat corruption. Progress will be difficult until the GoI enacts a Provincial Powers Law. Whether or not that law is passed, it appears that MoI IG has the budget sufficient to hire thousands of additional employees, many of whom would presumably man provincial offices.

MoI IG officials described their plan to field their presence in provincial or other branch offices of MoI. We noted that the plan had no corollary advisory linkage for officials both in the MoI HQ and within the provincial/branch offices of MoI. According to the MoI IG, the Iraqi MoI deals not only with policing issues, but also with birth records, death records, and most other official records touching the lives of Iraqi citizens.

MoI IG Comments. The MoI IG had served in previous post-Saddam Iraqi government positions. He said he served as the Minister of Women's Rights. As did virtually every Iraqi connected in any way with the ISF IG effort, he described himself as the eyes, ears, and

---

[9] Outside the International Zone.

conscience of his minister. He acknowledged that his office and the ministry had a long way to go to become an effective organization. He stated that his office hiring processes would yield sufficient numbers of new employees to carry out IG duties.

He was very pleased with his senior advisor and the advisory activity and asked for more advisory personnel, specifically noting he needed an advisor for audit. He also said that he needed a strong professional female to serve as a role model for the Iraqi female employees in his organization. He was a strong advocate to add more Iraqi women to the ministry's workforce.

Personnel. At the time of our visit, there were about 850 employees working in the IG office. Some employees were still on loan from (and being paid by) other departments within the ministry. The MoI IG had just received its independent budget and was responsible for paying office employees.

The MoI IG office was authorized 5,000 employees, and although the IG hoped to hire 1,500 additional employees by year's end, it was not clear how that goal would be accomplished. Within the MoI IG, neither the people nor the processes to support the necessary volume of centralized, merit-based hiring existed; therefore, such a plan was not realistic. Vetting candidates and predicting such factors as loyalty and qualifications would be a challenge.

Budget. The IG office's budget for supplies and equipment was described as "not even enough to supply the HQ, much less any provincial offices."

Audit. At the time of our visit, the MoI IG Audit component focused on paying the National Police. The Board of Supreme Audit (BSA) was providing oversight of the MoI's budget. Audit officials asserted that its efforts had returned 350 million Iraqi Dinar to the government. Officials identified the difficulties in providing an adequate audit function were similar to other areas in the MoI, e.g., shortages of personnel, limited office space/technology, and security/transportation restrictions that complicated travel to outlying MoI locations.

OIG Investigations - Internal Affairs. In addition to the Investigations function in the IG office, MoI had a separate Internal Affairs (IA) organization. According to both advisors and IG officials, the two functions were, for all practical purposes, indistinguishable. In describing the difference between his section's role and the role of IA, one Investigations' leader stated that IA did not have a clear guideline like CPA Order 57. IG Investigations leaders described their priority at the time as fighting administrative and financial corruption within MoI. Investigations were described as a very dangerous job. Four officers had been killed in the line of duty.

Inspections. Inspections personnel stated that the U.S.-style IG system represented a new way for the Iraqis to do inspections. The function was in the initial organizational stages. The Minister's order to return employees detailed to MOI IG back to their parent section was a major set back for the inspections office.

Human Rights. The Human Right function was relatively new to MoI IG. At the time of our visit, its mission was to inspect and report on detention facility conditions and to check records for numbers and identities of persons held in MOI custody. Advisory personnel confirmed that MoI IG leaders were very much engaged in the human rights areas. Still needed, however, was a set of written standards to effectively manage the detention centers. Without the security arrangements that accompany the presence of coalition advisors, the Iraqi members of the directorate indicated they would not be able to perform their required tasks.

IG Human Rights personnel described to us the existing Iraqi process by which Iraqi families could determine if a family member was being detained in a MoI facility. Leaders and personnel were eager to show us the computer database used to identify and track detainees. It was located on the single computer that was available to the directorate. The IG personnel acknowledged the rudimentary nature of the database and realized that more computers, equipment, and staffing would be required to improve access and use of the database.

Military-like organizations. The MoI's National Police Directorate is responsible for five units that, although characterized as police units, were organized, equipped, and operated much like military units. They included two National Police Divisions, a Mechanized National Police Brigade, a Quick Reaction Force, and an Emergency Response Unit. We did not detect any IG structure or policies that were suitable for inspection and oversight of those units.

Provincial Police. Planning and the ability to structure advisory efforts for Provincial-level activities was difficult without an approved Provincial Powers Law and a lack of published guidance. The precise duties and obligations of the Provincial Police Chiefs and their organizations to the MoI were unclear. Similarly, the obligations of MoI to Provincial Police Chiefs and/or power over them were vague and appeared to be in dispute. Those factors very much complicated MoI IG planning and also impeded the ability to structure advisory efforts for MoI IG provincial-level activities.

Other. Interestingly, conversations with some directorate-level leaders indicated their desire to be "independent," and not part of the MoI. The Commission on Public Integrity (CPI), the primary GoI criminal investigative arm, has made efforts to assert control over all ministerial IGs, urging them to be independent of the ministries and become a part of CPI.

Summary. The MoI OIG is not fully developed. The shortages of required personnel, transportation, technology, and lack of clear plans to correct these shortfalls will stymie the OIG's efforts to achieve a self-sustaining posture. A lack of clarity in how MoI IG will relate to the provincial police, even if resourced, presents additional challenges.

Iraqi National Counter-Terrorism Task Force IGs

At the time of the assessment, the Iraqis were developing two Counter-Terrorism (CT) elements.

The Counter-Terrorism Bureau (CTB) director, appointed by the Prime Minister (PM) with consent of the Council of Representatives (CoR), served as the principal advisor to the PM on CT matters. The CTB was responsible for strategy, policy, and priorities, as well as assignment of roles and responsibilities to supporting Ministries or agencies. Additionally, the CTB director provides civilian oversight of GoI CT efforts. The PM directive creating the CTB provided for an IG in the CTB. No additional information regarding structure or personnel authorization for the CTB IG office was available.

The Counter-Terrorism Command (CTC) was likewise in its early organizational stage. The CTC was a MoD organization designed to function at the level of the services and under the command of the MoD, but operationally under the control of the CTB. CTC was chartered in the military IG directive. It was authorized an IG and four additional personnel. No additional information regarding structure for the CTC IG office was available.

CT Advisory Structure. Near the end of our field work, a contractor arrived to provide advice to the CT IG. He was a retired military officer with substantial IG experience in the U.S. Special Operations Forces community.

Summary. Every aspect of IG structure, plans, and operations in the Iraqi CT community was too new to permit any meaningful observation except that it was encouraging to note that in creating the organizations, the Iraqi leadership had the foresight to include the IG function.

Conclusions

Positive Indicators

Development and Maturity of Iraqi Commitment to IG Systems. Two points portray an encouraging climate for a robust Iraqi ISF IG system:

First, MoD and MoI IGs have modified the structure of their organizations in response to priority needs in the current environment. For example, both IGs created a Human Rights Directorate as a mechanism to provide oversight over detainee operations. Such initiatives to change and grow to meet high priority challenges are signs that the IGs are taking ownership of their respective programs—an indicator that bodes well for continued development of the ISF IG system.

Second, literally every Iraqi ISF IG and staffer interviewed knew and recited that their purpose was to be the "eyes, ears, and conscience of their minister or commander." While merely parroting a phrase does not mean that an effective system has been built or that appropriate values have been inculcated, we concluded that the Iraqis' demonstrated ability to describe what responsibilities the individuals have and embrace constitutes a positive indicator of acceptance of the important tenets of economy, integrity, and efficiency in the ISF.

Advisory Operations. As noted, advisors are the primary DoD contributions to support the day-to-day advice and mentoring needs of the ISF IGs. At the time of our assessment, there was a mixture of government civilian employees, contractors, and uniformed military personnel as summarized in Figure 1. Overwhelmingly, the advisory corps was capable and experienced in the IG field and had established productive working relationships with their Iraqi counterparts and key staff members. Iraqi officials praised the advisors' support and contributions. As noted, there was a discernable level of turmoil in the MoD IG office when the IG was replaced. Nevertheless, our assessment team and advisors had lengthy and cordial meetings with the newly-selected MoD IG.

Advisor Relationships, Age, Maturity. In this cultural setting, maturity--age over rank--was an obvious plus in performing the advisors role. Another cultural consideration was the advisors ability to build personal relationships with the Iraqis and sustain those relationships over time. Short term advisor assignments, particularly for personnel without an extensive background in IG business, added little value to the advisory effort. Other desired advisor attributes included:

- Familiarity with local Iraqi customs and political savvy
- Post-graduate education

Need for integration of IG advisory activities. The demand for qualified, experienced advisors will continue as part of the U.S. strategy to help Iraq build the capacity for self-governance, particularly with the expansion of the IG system to the Army divisions and the provincial governments. Likewise, increased MOI oversight of the Iraqi Police will be needed as the police organization evolves and matures. These developments will require multi-command and interagency coordination. To facilitate and support an integrated approach, the Commander, MNSTC-I, created a command-level staff position for an IG Integrator.[10]

Concerns

Relief of IGs. To properly balance conclusions, it was noted that during the time the assessment team was on the ground in Iraq, the well-regarded Iraqi MoD IG was relieved of his duties and replaced. The replacement was a serving military general officer, who we observed to have the trust and confidence of the Minister of Defence.

The removal of the serving MoD IG and the relief of the civilian Acting MoD IG in 2005 and the subsequent suspension of IG activities, plus similar instances in MOI, underscores the need for additional education at the ministerial and higher levels regarding the need for both the appearance and the reality of acceptance of independent IGs, as called for by Iraqi law.

While we concur that communication, candor, and confidence between the minister/commander and the IG are needed for a properly functioning relationship, we submit that removal of IGs without scrupulous attention requirements of CPA Order 57 can raise questions about the ministers' compliance with the Iraqi law.

Ministerial Ability to Block Prosecutions. Some Iraqi and U.S. officials complained that a provision of Iraqi law regarding prosecutions of government employees, known as "Section 136B," is a substantial impediment to prosecuting corruption. Section 136B provides for a suspension of prosecution of ministerial subordinates unless the relevant minister over-turns the suspension.

The argument for repeal of Section 136B relies on the assumption that the Iraqi judicial process is adequately insulated from influences that motivate corruption in other elements of Iraqi society.

To be sure, there are courageous and independent Iraqi judges doing their duty in the face of threats and coercion, just as there are courageous Iraqis in all walks of life who similarly resist intimidation and undue influence. Particularly among civilian employees at the MoD, there was sentiment that past corruption cases have swept up innocent employees along with those deserving of prosecution.

Even though ultimately cleared, blameless MoD employees endured lengthy incarcerations while awaiting resolution of their cases, according to anecdotes frequently recited. The perception that such an experience could easily befall innocent staffers contributes to a reluctance of civilian employees to assume the responsibilities for their assigned functions.

---

[10] We were advised that the position was filled with an experienced USMC IG-qualified colonel who worked to build capacity in ISF and Iraq IG systems; particularly significant given that MNSTC-I was without a command IG who might otherwise serve as a center of gravity for ISF IG advisory efforts. The integrator's position has evolved into the MNSTC-I command IG's position.

The elaborate measures to protect the few judges working at the "Rule of Law Green Zone" would seem to suggest that, absent special measures, judges and the judicial process are at risk, and subject to the same pressures and dangers, as are seen as corrupting to other segments of Iraqi society and government. Unfettered ministerial power to block prosecutions is clearly not good if invoked for improper motives. However, the perception that unfettered power to prosecute has been, and might continue to be, used for corrupt or partisan purposes appears to hinder capacity building efforts, at least in the MoD.

Training Challenges

Iraqi Concerns on Training. Iraqis expressed the need for more training to improve duty performance and to accelerate the development of the ISF IG system. A common theme during our discussions with Iraqi personnel was the desire to attend training at out-of-Iraq locations.

ISF IG Personnel Lack Experience. Many of the Iraqi IG personnel are managing or leading at organizational levels without the pre-requisite experience or qualifications. While the IGs of both MoD and MoI were exposed to cultures outside Iraq during the Saddam era, many on their respective staffs had no management or leadership training; hence, such training was frequently requested.

Selecting Training Locations. While there may be social-political, educational, and cultural advantages to attending training programs outside Iraq, pragmatic and logistical considerations suggest the best option is to conduct training in-country or in friendly nations in the region. Advisors pointed to the difficulties involved to obtain visas and arrange transportation and logistics for out-of-country training. Perhaps more significantly, advisors, familiar with the military maxim that people or organizations should "train as you fight," questioned the return on theoretical training delivered in a non-Iraqi environment. The need is to administer a training program that is directly related and tailored to deal with the immediate day-to-day issues confronting ISF IG personnel in Iraq's unique environment.

Regional Training and Relations. Our assessment team was advised that the original 2004 formal training for 640 Iraqi IG staff members was conducted at the Sadat Management Institute in Cairo, Egypt. As noted in a 2006 SIGIR report, the Arab Organization of Supreme Audit Institutes is active in the region. Furthermore, the Kingdom of Morocco has previously made an audit training offer, and international organizations, such as the World Bank and the United Nations, have participated in training efforts in-country.[11] These sources not only provide training, but also promote opportunities for Iraqi officials to interface in a positive way with their regional counterparts.

Delivery and Sustainment of Professional Anticorruption Training. Given the need for professional training across the GoI spectrum of ministries and organizations, establishing a centralized training institution has merit.

---

[11] Special IG for Iraq Reconstruction Report No. SIGIR-06-21, "Joint Survey of Anticorruption Programs, Embassy Baghdad, Iraq," July 28, 2006, p.6.

Auditors are employed in the IG offices, on the Board of Supreme Audit, throughout the GoI ministries. Likewise, investigators are employed in ISF and non-ISF ministries, the Commission on Public Integrity, and in a myriad of police and security organizations. Inspectors are employed throughout the government.

Furthermore, the inspection function existed in the former Iraqi military. Indeed, a number of the officials that were serving in the MoI and MoD IG offices had considerable experience as inspectors under that system. In addition to the Human Rights and detainee-rights work being done in the ISF ministries, there is an entirely separate Ministry of Human Rights in the GoI.

Concomitantly, the ubiquitous turf protection and stove-piping present in all bureaucratic governments has resulted in each Iraqi ministry doing its own training arrangements. Professional training required to be competent in the basic IG job functions is common across many GoI institutions and across the ISF. To the extent possible, leveraging common training opportunities across the ISF ministries should be the model.

A number of talented advisors, both contractors and government employees, have delivered training to segments of the ISF IG community. Though judged to be successful initiatives, such *ad hoc* training arrangements were limited in scope. They did not offer the most efficient model for delivering training and did not give the Iraqis institutional ownership for their training program. Instead, the preferred alternative is a centralized institution to deliver training in a consistent, efficient, and economical manner. Such an initiative has been endorsed repeatedly by the Iraqi leadership and there is support to create an Iraqi Academy of Principled Governance or a similar multi-ministry national training entity.

While DoD may not have the U.S. lead for such an initiative, DoD activities and resources are being directed at training efforts. MoD Transition Team advisors have facilitated the start of a training academy for MoD civilians. At the time of this assessment, a new contractor was in-bound to be an IG trainer for the MoD

A previous SIGIR report described the need for Embassy Baghdad and the Bureau of International Narcotics and Law Enforcement Affairs to support "Iraqi efforts to design and establish a training facility for anti-corruption personnel from, and with the support of, all three institutions of the Iraqi anti-corruption structure."[12]

Over several years, such an initiative has been endorsed repeatedly by much of the Iraqi leadership, though perhaps referred to by different names at different times. In addition to having been the subject of recommendations from IGs, both Iraqi and U.S., it is the critical Iraqi national mechanism to sustain, professionalize, and coordinate anti-corruption. The substance of the SIGIR recommendation applies with equal force to DoD elements in Iraq.

Vigorous U.S. support for such a professional sustaining mechanism, and leadership from DoD organizations for that support, is vital to sustain the IG and other anti-corruption efforts in the Iraqi security ministries and the GoI. The value of one national training entity to assist Iraqi anti-

---

[12]Ibid, p.8.

corruption personnel in becoming more professional and in lessening the pernicious effects of sectarianism has also been recognized by experts from the academic world.[13]

Other Factors Regarding Centralization of Anticorruption Training. While USAID supports Iraqi civil servant training programs, MNSTC-I advisory personnel and their Iraqi counterparts stated that ISF IG personnel have not participated in USAID training venues.

Efficiency and Avoidance of Unintended Messages. An additional consideration supporting the centralization of training efforts is to avoid unintended consequences when significant coalition support is directed to only certain ministries or agencies. Given the very prevalent perception, if not the reality, that certain ministries or agencies were dominated by one sect or party, it is evident that training dollars, school seats, or other advantages devoted to only one ministry can easily be construed as supporting certain sectarian interests over others. Training centralization at the highest possible level achieves not only economies of scale, but also avoids unintended involvement with sectarian interests, which serve to fragment the GoI. One also expects that donor nations and Non-Governmental Organizations desiring to engage with Iraq on good governance and anti-corruption issues will be more willing and able to contribute through a central national institution, as contrasted with negotiating arrangements with individual ministries and agencies.

Prognosis for Success

As to the ISF IG systems, there are some very good top-line indicators and some less satisfactory indicators. It is deemed positive that there is both acceptance of the IG concept and progress toward building capacity to do the job throughout the ISF IG systems, despite the fact that such systems, and the concepts behind them, are quite alien to Iraqi experience. Given the great volume of that which needs to be done, the systems are very much a work in progress and likely to take years to mature.

USG Transition and Capacity-Building Relating to ISF IG Systems

Joint Iraqi Army and Police Operations. During the fieldwork for this assessment, Operation, Fardh Al-Qanoon was underway in Baghdad. The "Baghdad Operations Command" was organized and tailored to operate as a joint Iraqi Army-Iraqi Police command. During the operations, substantial numbers of prisoners were taken into custody by elements of both the Army and Police. The Human Rights Directorates of both MoD and MoI OIGs were involved in monitoring detention operations of their respective ministries. Doctrine and planning to accommodate IG operations in Iraqi joint operations had not been developed. Because joint

---

[13] Commenting on steps for "(d)e-corrupting Iraqi Security Forces," Dr. Charles Moskos has observed that oversight is necessary and that members engaged in oversight, "...can be recruited to attend a special academy. The academy would stress professional over sectarian identity, the service ethic over pecuniary motives and, very important, be headed by honest mentors." Charles Moskos , "American Military Interaction with Locals in Operation Iraqi Freedom (OIF)," Technical Report for U.S. Army Research Institute for the Behavioral and Social Sciences, Addendum, p.19, March 2007.

operations are likely to increase in frequency and importance, commanders and IGs should develop the policies and procedures to execute and manage these types of emerging needs.

MNSTC-I Transition to OSC-I. At the time of this assessment, MNSTC-I was developing plans for the "Office of Security Cooperation-Iraq "(OSC-I), which would be the follow-on organization to continue the capacity building process for the security ministries. Timing for transition to OSC-I was not fixed and was condition-based. Accordingly, OSC-I would continue to help foster an ethos in "ISF ministries to serve as professional and model institutions of Iraqi National Unity" and to help "set conditions for long term self-sustainment."[14]

We were told that the proposal for the OSC-I organization was yet to be finalized. Some briefings did not clearly delineate an IG mentoring function with the MoD and MoI headquarters. We contend that the advisory and mentoring functions should continue going forward.[15]

Resourcing the Multi-National Corps – Iraq (MNC-I) IG Advisory Effort. The MNC-I IG took aggressive steps to support capacity building in the ISF military units and created a liaison position on his staff to facilitate the interface between the IG advisory and mentoring assets to the newly-created Iraqi military IGs. As the repository for IG expertise in MNC-I, he was the logical center of gravity for this effort.

It does not appear that there is doctrinal guidance on whether a corps IG should provide IG advice/mentoring to host-nation partnership organizations, such as a Service-level headquarters and partnered divisions. In this instance, the responsible corps IG has, very appropriately, presumed that as the trained and experienced subject matter expert in IG issues, he was the source for advice/mentoring to his corps' partnered Iraqi units.

Doctrine should exist to guide future corps or division IGs confronted with that situation so that appropriate resourcing for the responsibility can be planned and provided. Headquarters that succeed to the MNC-I mission of partnering and mentoring IGFC headquarters and divisions with an IG capability should follow the lead of the MNC-I IG serving at the time of this assessment in addressing that mission even absent interim or final doctrinal guidance.

Embassy Working Group Participation. Integration of the anti-corruption plans and IG advisory activities of MNF-I and subordinate units with all U.S.-led anti-corruption activity took place in Embassy Working Groups, specifically the "Anti-Corruption Working Group" (ACWG). The MNSTC-I senior IG advisor attended the ACWG meetings.[16] If that is the forum in which significant governance and anti-corruption activities are to be harmonized, MNSTC-I and MNF-I must be active participants.[17]

The MNF-I staff section listed as a participant in the ACWG was Strategic Effects. When contacted during field work, a representative of that office stated that, although an officer had been present as an observer at meetings of the ACWG, the Strategic Effects representative "did

---

[14]Briefing, MNSTC-I, "Proposed Office of Security Cooperation-Iraq," 29 May 2007.

[15] Subsequent to this assessment, CG MNSTC-I provided for the continuation of an IG advisory effort for the ISF IGs.

[16] The advisor also attended the "Rule of Law Working Group" meetings.

[17] The assessment team did not address the effectiveness of the particular meetings that the team observed.

not have a seat at the table." MNF-I and its subordinate elements must do more than observe if that working group coordination forum is to be meaningful.

Given the experience and resources DoD brings to bear on this topic in Iraq, MNF-I should seek to have a prominent role in the ACWG and like entities. Prior SIGIR recommendations that this should be at the senior-officer level are consistent with the observed need. It is noted that the SIGIR recommendation called for a senior "leader."

"Rule of Law." In addition to the usual bureaucratic and human impediments to coordination, it appears that efforts to coordinate issues critical to advising Iraqi IGs at the ministerial level may be dogged by differences in usages assigned to the term "Rule of Law."

The Embassy upward reporting chain for the one non-security IG advisor to the 27 non-security ministry IGs was to the Embassy Office of Accountability and Transparency (OAT). OAT reported to the Embassy Rule of Law Coordinator. In MNF-I and its subordinate military units, neither IGs nor IG advisors reported to the command lawyer or Judge Advocate.

In analyzing and discussing "rule of law" issues in the Embassy setting, it appeared that the full range of IG, anti-corruption, economy and efficiency, and good governance issues were implicated. In contrast, in MNF-I, it appears that rule of law issues were basically the province of Judge Advocates. The broad range of IG issues that do not directly involve law enforcement, judicial proceedings, and sentencing considerations apparently did not fall within common usage of the term "rule of law," as observed in MNSTC-I.

The issue is of more than academic interest in a setting in which the forum to coordinate and communicate issues is the embassy working group. Embassy rule of law as well as Embassy ACWG meetings were attended and observed. The intersection of Embassy and MNF-I working-level coordination on anti-corruption and rule of law issues would be assisted by careful examination of what the differences mean, if differing definitions are, in fact, intended to be used.

Doctrine for IG Advisory Functions in Support to Security, Stability, Transition, and Reconstruction (SSTR) Operations. Personnel resources to perform the national-level ISF ministry IG advisory mission have, over the history of the Iraqi ISF IG advisory mission, been provided from three sources: contractors, uniformed military personnel, and government civilian employees.

The assessment team was aware from interviews with advisors and others, that DoD-level civilian employees from a number of different DoD offices have been, at various times, detailed or otherwise provided to MNSTC-I or other organizations to participate in advising Iraqi national ministry-level officials. It is evident that such personnel, who have subject matter expertise in U.S. national-level defense functions, should be suited to provide advice to the host nation in developing its own national-level defense capacity in their areas of expertise.

DoD has established an Office of Stability Operations Capabilities to, among other responsibilities, lead DoD efforts to implement DoD Directive 3000.05, "Military Support for Stability, Security, Transition, and Reconstruction (SSTR) Operations," and to identify and bridge the gaps in stability operations capability, capacity, and compatibility within DoD.[18] Numerous SSTR-related activities directed toward formulating appropriate doctrine are underway. It is likely to be a long time for those activities to be completed and yield final DoD-level policies and guidance on personnel resourcing for SSTR missions. It may be that interim guidance regarding national-level advisory missions for ongoing operations in Iraq would be appropriate. If it is a responsibility of DoD-level staff to provide personnel for ongoing advisory missions, then the plans and resourcing requests at MNSTC-I (or a successor Office of Security Cooperation) and at contributing DoD staff elements will be better informed if interim guidance is articulated.

> It will take time to develop the governmental institutions of Iraq, including the anti-corruption system. Open and transparent government is a concept which will take time to become permanent.
>
> Layla Jassim al-Mokthar, IG Iraqi MoD,
> Remarks before the President's Council on Integrity and Efficiency,
> Washington, DC, 12 July 2005

---

[18] " DoD Report to Congress on the Implementation of DoD Directive 3000.05, "Military Support for Stability, Security, Transition, and Reconstruction (SSTR) Operations," April 1, 2007.

Considerations for the Future

Based on our observations, the following considerations for the future are noted:

CONSIDERATION 1: Establishment of an Iraqi National Academy of Principled Governance or similar institution as a training facility for anti-corruption personnel from, and with the support of, all three institutions of the Iraqi anti-corruption structure is a sensible and efficient vehicle to coordinate the use of training resources across ISF IG and associated IG systems. Economy, efficiency, and professionalism are well-served by centralizing training for the national anticorruption and oversight organizations. Development of a centralized training program for uniformed IGs in the military IG system is similarly significant.

CONSIDERATION 2: Iraqi joint police and military operations occur frequently. ISF IG activities, including detainee operations oversight, benefit from coalition advisory/mentoring assistance to Iraqi security ministries, commanders, and staffs as they prepare ISF joint operational plans, policies, and procedures.

CONSIDERATION 3: DoD guidance for provision of IG advisory/mentoring activities to host-nation security establishments, such as the Iraqi Security Ministries, Joint and Service-level headquarters, and partnered security units does not exist. Whether that mission is an appropriate role for U.S. Joint Task Force/Corps/Division or other IGs is not clear.

CONSIDERATION 4: Continued provision of advisory resources and activities to support development of all ISF IG systems, to include military IG system in the Iraqi Ground Forces Command and Iraqi Army divisions, as well as the Air Force and the Navy, is important to the growth of a culture of efficiency and accountability in the ISFs.

CONSIDERATION 5: An Anticorruption Working Group (ACWG) hosted at Embassy Baghdad has served as the forum in which significant governance and anti-corruption activities are harmonized among the interested coalition agencies. Advisory assistance to the IG systems in the security ministries that is consistent with a comprehensive coalition anticorruption strategy is important. Active participation in the ACWG by MNSTC-I and MNF-I officers of appropriate rank is important to that effort.

Appendix A: Scope and Methodology

Scope

This assessment was a self-initiated evaluation of DoD's support to assist the Iraqi MoD, MoI, and Joint Headquarters (JHQ) IGs in establishing a self-sustaining IG function under Iraqi law. The assessment focused on the operations, plans and projected needs of these ISF IGs organizations within the context of the U.S. Government's transition and capacity-building goals as well as Iraqi anti-corruption strategies and objectives.

The assessment team did not examine the process by which policy decisions were reached on structure of the ISF IG system, nor the policy decisions themselves. As with all reconstruction, stabilization, and capacity-building efforts in Iraq, the coalition programs to develop the ISF, including the various IGs, are continually evolving.

Methodology

From April through August 2007, the IG assessment team performed the following steps:

- Reviewed applicable directives and policies governing support to the ISF IG programs.

- Conducted interviews with senior U.S. government officials responsible for the program, including personnel of the Departments of State and Defense.

- Conducted fieldwork and interviews with senior civilian and military officials of the US, Coalition, and Iraqi governments.

- Interviewed non-government officials.

- Visited U.S., Iraqi and Coalition personnel and facilities in Iraq, to include Camp Victory, the International Zone including the Iraqi MoD Headquarters Building, Forward Operating Base (FOB) Honor, Old Muthana Air Base, FOB Shield, Baghdad Police College and the MoI Headquarters building in the Rusafa district; also the 10th Iraqi Army Division Headquarters at Basra, Taji Air Base/ National Depot, and the Iraqi Naval Base at Umm Qsar.

- Conducted exit briefs with senior officials in Iraq.

Communication with Iraqi personnel was often through interpreters. Some interpreters were provided by the ISF organizations with which contact took place; others were supplied by MNSTC-I or other U.S. government entities. Communications reported in this assessment were judged sufficiently reliable from context, documents, or other circumstances for use in the assessment. A very considerable number of Iraqi officials communicated with the assessment team in the English language.

Appendix B: The Government of the Republic of Iraq

The Coalition Provisional Authority (CPA) disbanded on June 28, 2004, transferring sovereign authority for governing Iraq to the Iraqi Interim Government (IIG). Based on the timetable laid out in the Transitional Administrative Law, the IIG governed Iraq until the January 30, 2005, elections. Thereafter, the Iraqi Transitional Government assumed authority.

The Iraqi Transitional Government-drafted constitution was finalized in September 2005 and ratified in a nationwide referendum on October 15, 2005. On December 15, 2005, Iraqis voted in the first legislative elections prescribed by the new constitution. The new four-year, constitutionally based government took office in March 2006, and the new cabinet was approved and installed in May 2006.

The legislative branch is a 275-member elected Council of Representatives (CoR). The Iraqi structure provides that the President, along with two Deputies, form the Presidency Council. The Presidency Council appoints the Prime Minister who appoints the Council of Ministers (cabinet), all of whom must be approved by the CoR. The Prime Minister (PM) holds most of the executive authority under the official structure of the Government of Iraq (GoI). The Prime Minister is Commander-in-Chief of the armed forces. Iraq also has an independent judiciary.

At the time of our field work, the GoI structure called for 31 ministries for the national-level government. Key among those with responsibility for the security of Iraq were the Ministries of Defence and Interior.

It is significant to note that with the changes in government from Interim to Transitional to permanent, the people occupying positions of senior leadership in the Iraqi government, including Ministers of Defence and Interior, changed.

Republic of Iraq – Ministry of Defence
CPA Order No. 2 dissolved the Saddam-era Ministry of Defence, as it existed prior to the regime change, in its entirety. CPA Order No. 67, effective March 21, 2004, created the new Iraqi MoD.

The new MoD provides civilian control of the Iraqi Armed Forces and supporting organizations. The MoD has the responsibility of defending the borders and protecting the people and interests of Iraq against external and internal threats, in cooperation with other ministries and the GoI.

MoD forces consist of the Joint Headquarters (JHQ), the Iraqi Ground Forces Command (the Iraqi Army), the Iraqi Special Operations Forces (ISOF), the Iraqi Air Force, and the Iraqi Navy.

The Iraqi military had an authorized strength of approximately 175,000 personnel and centered on an Army with nine infantry divisions, one mechanized infantry division, and associated combat support units. The PM's Expansion Initiative, underway during our assessment, provided for expansion of the Army by development of two additional infantry divisions. The Iraqi Air

Force consisted of six squadrons; the Iraqi Navy had two squadrons and a Marine battalion. In addition to this PM's approved expansion, Iraqi personnel at all levels indicate that further growth in the size of the Iraqi military was expected.

MoD was organized into approximately a dozen functional directorates to accomplish its mission.

Republic of Iraq – Joint Headquarters
Command of the Iraqi military was exercised through the civilian Minister of Defense. His senior uniformed subordinate was an Iraqi four-star general, the Chief of Staff Joint Forces. JHQ was part of the MoD and was responsible for the command and control of Iraqi Joint Forces, including the Iraqi Army, the Air Force, the Navy, as well as the Iraqi Special Operations Forces (ISOF). The JHQ was comprised of a traditional military staff organization with coordinating and special staffs.

Republic of Iraq – Ministry of the Interior
The MoI was responsible, among many other duties, for the internal security of Iraq and for the provision of emergency response organizations and facilities protection services. It had both criminal and domestic intelligence capabilities, and it regulated private security companies operating in Iraq. The ministry had many non-law enforcement records responsibilities.

The MoI commanded a number of uniformed forces, including the National Police, Department of Border Enforcement, and Bureau of Dignitary Protection. MoI also ran the Iraqi Civil Defense Directorate (Iraq's firefighters and emergency response organization). In addition, MoI oversaw and set standards for the Facilities Protection Service. It also had significant responsibilities for the Iraqi Police Service.

The MoI was organized pursuant to MoI Structural Law (Part III, Article 10-31, Law No. 11, 1994). Some independent directorates and departments were added as a result of CPA Orders and Memoranda. A new Structural Law for the MoI was currently pending before the Council of Representatives.

At the time of this assessment, the MoI headquarters consisted of the Minister's Office, eight independent directorates (National Police; Weapons, Cards and Badges; Travel/Nationality; Internal Affairs; General Counsel; Operations; Contract; and IG) and five departments headed by deputy ministers (Support Forces; Financial Affairs; Administration; National Information & Investigations Agency; and Iraqi Police Service Affairs and Security).

Iraqi National Counter-Terrorism Force
Iraq had recently provided for a National Counter-Terrorism (CT) Capability. Approved by the PM on October 10, 2006, the National CT Capability included two main components: the Counter-Terrorism Bureau (CTB) and the Counter-Terrorism Command (CTC).

The CTB was separate from the ministries. Appointed by the PM with consent from the Council of Representatives, the CTB Director advised the PM on CT and developed GoI CT strategy, policy, and priorities. Furthermore, he assigned roles and responsibilities as part of the strategic planning duties in supporting ministries or agencies. The CTB Director provided civilian oversight of MoD CT efforts.

The CT Command was equivalent to the ground, air, and naval forces commands. It provided support to the CTB in areas of intelligence and targeting. Providing a nation-wide capability to interdict the high-value terrorist targets, the CTC's precise relationships to the JHQ, the CTB, and the PM's office were evolving during this assessment. Different documents and briefings we reviewed varied in the details of those relationships. A component of the CTC was the subordinate ISOF Brigade, a part of the MoD. The ISOF Brigade was the operational component of the CTC.

Government of Iraq Anti-Corruption Entities
Collectively, the Iraqi IGs constituted one of the three "Pillars of Anti-Corruption." The other two pillars were the Board of Supreme Audit (BSA) and the Commission on Public Integrity (CPI).

Prior to 2004, there was no history of a Federal IG system in Iraq, or other countries in the Middle East. In 2004, the CPA created the CPI, the Iraqi IG System, and reconstituted the BSA through the promulgation of CPA orders 55, 57, and 77, respectively. The BSA and CPI were independent bodies.

The CPI served as the primary investigative law enforcement body for allegations of corruption. It developed and tracked a Code of Conduct that was signed by all state employees; developed and tracked Financial Disclosure Forms filed by senior public officials; and promoted "transparency in government" programs to enhance public access to information about government contracts and operations. The commissioner of the CPI reported to the Iraqi PM.

The BSA served as an independent audit body, informed the public and government, and promoted economy and efficiency. BSA undertook financial and performance audits and program evaluations. It promulgated auditing and accounting regulations, drafted to international standards and provides quality oversight of IG audits. The President of the Board of Audit also reported to the PM.

Iraq's ministries carried out many of the executive functions of government. The security ministries were the MoD and MoI. CPA Order 57 prescribes the duties of all ministry-level Iraqi "federal" IGs. The order was in effect at the time sovereignty passed to the GoI in June of 2004. It is among those orders that remain Iraqi law.[1]

---

[1] Except as it relates to flow of funding directly to the IGs, CPA Order 57 remains unchanged since its promulgation.

Change 1 to CPA 57 provides for an "independent budget" for all IGs. Funding in the future will be provided directly to the federal offices of IG from the Minister of Finance, rather than from the respective ministries. That independent funding provides a degree of financial and practical independence for the IGs.

In considering ISF IGs, it is to be noted that only the two ministerial-level IGs, MoD and MoI, were created by CPA Order 57. The military IGs (JHQ, Army, Navy, and Air Force, together with the IGs in subordinate commands and each of the Army divisions) were subsequently created by administrative direction of the Minister of Defence. The IGs in the CTB and Command were created separately in the authorizations relating to those CT entities.

The concept of the IG as an extension of the eyes, ears, and conscience of the military commander or minister appears largely a U.S.-unique construct. When CPA introduced the IG concept, the basic IG organizational model suggested to GoI officials was the same functional organization seen in most federal-level IGs in the United States. That model provided for three major functions: Inspections, Investigations, and Audit.

CPA Order 57 recognizes that Iraq's former regime fostered inefficiency and corruption in governmental institutions and that a concerted effort was needed to restore public trust and confidence in the institutions of government.

Although not provided for in any official sense, the national-level IGs who were appointed pursuant to the CPA orders organized an Association of IGs. From among their numbers, those federal-level IGs select an IG to serve as the head of the association and as its spokesman. That association has met monthly since introduction of the IG system to the ministries. It served as a forum for not only the IGs, but also for representatives of the other Iraqi Anti-Corruption Agencies to communicate and coordinate on a wide variety of issues. The head of the association at the time of this assessment was the IG of the Ministry of Health. The head of the IG association, on behalf of the IGs, had initiated a process of inspecting the various ministerial IG offices to promote efficiency and progress within its own ranks.

The GoI created a national-level Joint Anti-Corruption Council (JACC), formed on May 16, 2006. The JACC was designed to coordinate anti-corruption agencies and formulate nationwide strategies to combat corruption. Members of the JACC were the Secretary of the Council of Ministers, a representative of the Iraqi Higher Juridical Council, a senior member of the organization of Iraqi IGs, the President of the BSA, and the Commissioner of the CPI.

The concepts of governmental transparency and accountability are new to most Iraqis. The assessment team was advised that Saddam-era Iraqi military and police experiences with a "General Inspector" was a position that carried the power to reward or to punish in a corrupt system. It was reported that some Iraqis viewed the establishment of the IG program as reimplementation of that former General Inspector system. The cultural baggage associated with the former General Inspector has likely provided challenges to education of Iraqis at all levels on the positive aspects of the new IG system.

Appendix C: Multi-National Security Transition Command-Iraq

Multi-National Security Transition Command-Iraq. The structure through which almost all direct advisory support was provided is the Multi-National Security Transition Command-Iraq (MNSTC-I), which was a subordinate command of the Multi-National Force – Iraq (MNF-I). MNSTC-I was formed to assist the Iraqi Government in the development, organization, training, equipping, and mentoring of the ISFs of the MoD and MoI. At the command level, MNSTC-I had a coordinating and special staff. MNSTC-I was not authorized an IG and one was not assigned. IG coverage for the command was provided by the MNF-I IG.

MNSTC-I Organizational Chart

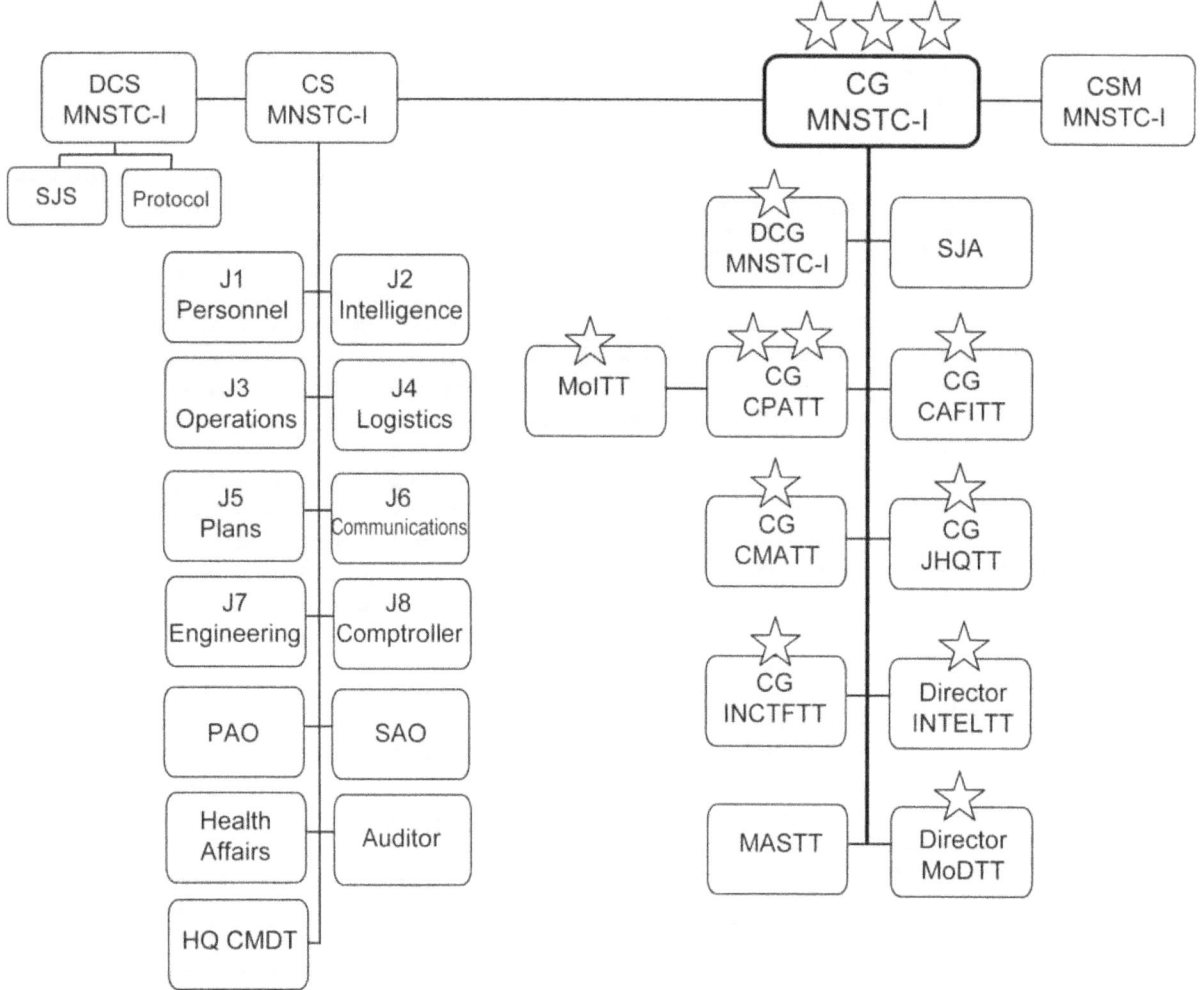

Figure 5: MNSTC-I Organization Chart. (Source: MNSTC-I.)

MNSTC-I described its operations as taking place through subordinate transition teams. Among those teams were:

1. **Coalition Military Assistance Training Team (CMATT)** supported the Iraqi Ministry of Defence (MoD) and Joint Headquarters (JHQ) to recruit, train, equip, base, and sustain Iraqi Army, Air Force, and Navy units throughout Iraq. CMATT included the Ministry of Defence Transition Team (MoD-TT). The MoD-TT was partnered with Iraq's MoD to assist in the development of Iraq's military capacity and its ability to lead and resource the Iraqi Armed Forces. Advisors to the MoD IG were assigned to the MoD-TT.

2. **Joint Headquarters Transition Team (JHQ-TT)** was partnered with the JHQ to assist in the development of Iraq's JHQ inside the MoD to effectively command and control the Iraqi Joint Forces, which included the Army, the Navy, and the Air Force. Advisors to the JHQ IG were assigned to the JHQ-TT.

3. **Civilian Police Assistance Training Team (CPATT)** which, in partnership with the Iraqi Government, was responsible for training, equipping, organizing, mentoring and developing the MoI forces to include the Iraqi Police Service, National Police forces, Emergency Response Unit, Department of Border Enforcement, and Dignitary Protection.

4. **Ministry of the Interior Transition Team (MoI-TT)** was partnered with Iraq's MoI to assist in the development of Iraq's law enforcement capacity and its ability to lead and resource the Iraqi Police. Advisors to the MoI IG were assigned to the MoI-TT.

5. **Iraqi National Counter-Terrorism Task Force Transition Team (INCTF-TT)** had the mission to establish, organize, train, equip and advise the Iraqi National Counter-Terrorism Task Force. The advisor to the Counter-Terrorism Bureau IG was assigned to the INCTF-TT.

Appendix D: Multi-National Corps-Iraq

MNC-I was the tactical unit responsible for command and control of operations throughout Iraq. Among its subordinate units were a number of division headquarters. It was a subordinate command of MNF-I. MNC-I headquarters, as well as the subordinate divisions that were U.S. divisional headquarters, had organic IGs assigned to their staffs.

MNC-I's Iraq Assistance Group was the parent organization for Military Transition Teams (MiTTs). Those MiTTs provided advisory support and access to coalition military assets for the Iraqi Army battalions, brigades, and divisions with which the MiTTs were partnered,

Recognizing that the development of an IG system in the Iraqi Ground Forces Command and the Iraqi Army Divisions presented the need for advice and mentoring, the MNC-I IG proactively secured approval for a position on his joint manning document for an IG-qualified officer to serve as an advisor and mentor. That position provides an officer to advise and mentor Iraqi IGs as well as to facilitate contact among Iraqi and coalition divisional IGs and MiTTs. The MNC-I IG advisor also eases communication with the MNSTC-I IG advisors working with the JHQ and MoD IGs. That insightful action by the MNC-I IG provided critical linkage between the efforts of MNSTC-I advisors working at the JHQ and MoD levels and the MNC-I advisory efforts. The process of providing extra eyes and ears for both Iraqi and coalition commanders through those IGs and advisors should be of significant value in building capacity in the Iraqi units and on many other levels as well.

As the mission has continued, the MNC-I responsibilities have passed with transition of authority to different U.S. Army corps headquarters. Succeeding headquarters will require resources beyond those normally available to a corps headquarters or a corps IG in order to perform the IG advisory and coordination mission necessary to maintain momentum in the development of the IG system within the Iraqi Army organizations with which MNC-I is partnered.

Appendix E: Organizations and Acronyms

AC	Anti-Corruption
ACWG	Anti-Corruption Working Group
BSA	Board of Supreme Audit
CoS	Chief of Staff (CoS)
CPI	Commission on Public Integrity
CT	Counter-Terrorism
CTB	Counterterrorism Bureau
DG	Director General
GOI	Government of Iraq
IAD	Iraqi Army Division
IGFC	Iraqi Ground Forces Command
INCTF-TT	Iraqi National Counter-Terrorism Force Transition Team
IRMO	Iraq Reconstruction Management Office
ISF	Iraq Security Forces (military & police)
ISOF	Iraqi Special Operations Forces
JACC	Joint Anti-Corruption Council
JHQ	Joint Headquarters
JHQ-TT	Joint Headquarters Transition Team
MiTT	Military Transition Team
MNF-I	Multi-National Force – Iraq
MNSTC-I	Multi-National Security Transition Command – Iraq
MNC-I	Multi-National Corps – Iraq
MOD	Ministry of Defence
MOD-TT	Ministry of Defence Transition Team
MOI	Ministry of Interior
MOI-TT	Ministry of Interior Transition Team
MPRI	There is no translation for this. It is a military contractor which provides (among other things) advisors for MNSTC-I's advisory work in Iraq.
OAT	Office of Accountability and Transparency
OSC	Office of Security Cooperation
PM	Prime Minister
PRT	Provincial Reconstruction Team
SIGIR	Special IG for Iraq Reconstruction
TT	Transition Team - the advisory teams in MNSTC-I for MoD, MOI, and JHQ.

Appendix F: Distribution List

Department of Defense

Office of the Secretary of Defense
Under Secretary of Defense for Policy
Assistant Secretary of Defense for Special Operations & Low Intensity Conflict
Principal Director, Stability Operations

Joint Chiefs of Staff
Inspector General, Joint Staff
Director for Operations (J-3)
Director for Force Structure, Resources & Assessment (J-8)

Combatant Commands
Commander, U.S. Central Command
      Inspector General, U.S. Central Command
      Commander, Multi-National Force – Iraq
            Inspector General, Multi-National Force – Iraq
            Commander, Multi-National Security Transition Command – Iraq
            Inspector General, Multi-National Security Transition Command- Iraq
            Commander, Multi-National Corps – Iraq
            Inspector General, Multi-National Corps - Iraq
Inspector General, U.S. Africa Command
Inspector General, U.S. European Command
Inspector General, U.S. Joint Forces Command
Inspector General, U.S. Pacific Command
Inspector General, U.S. Southern Command

Department of State
Inspector General

Embassies
U.S. Embassy, Baghdad, Iraq
Ambassador
Deputy Chief of Mission
Coordinator for Anticorruption Initiatives

Other Federal Organizations
Government Accountability Office
Special Inspector General for Iraq Reconstruction

Congressional Committees and Subcommittees, Chairman and Ranking Minority Member

Senate Subcommittee on Defense, Committee on Appropriations
Senate Committee on Armed Services
Senate Committee on Foreign Relations
Senate Committee on Homeland Security and Governmental Affairs
Senate Select Committee on Intelligence
House Subcommittee on Defense, Committee on Appropriations
House Committee on Armed Services
House Committee on Foreign Affairs
House Committee on Oversight and Government Reform
House Subcommittee on National Security and Foreign Affairs,
    Committee on Oversight and Government Affairs
House Permanent Select Committee on Intelligence

THE MISSION OF THE OIG DOD

The Office of the IG promotes integrity, accountability, and improvement of DoD personnel, programs, and operations to support the Department's mission and to serve the public interest.

TEAM MEMBERS

The Inspections and Evaluations Directorate, Office of the Deputy IG for Policy and Oversight of the DoD IG prepared this report. Personnel who contributed to the report include Mr. Deane Williams – Division Chief, Mr. John G. Townsend – Project Leader, and COL (P) Nickolas P. Tooliatos (USAR).

ADDITIONAL REPORT COPIES

Contact us by phone, fax, or e-mail:
   Inspections and Evaluations directorate, Deputy IG for Policy and Oversight
   COM: 703.604.9130 (DSN664.9130)
   FAX: 703.604.9769
   E-MAIL: crystalfocus@dodig.mil
   Electronic version available at: www.dodig.mil/Inspections/IE/Reports